YOUR KNOWLEDGE HAS VALUE

AF136424

Increasing Public Engagement On The Issue of Nuclear Waste In The USA. Defense Paper

Madison Alvarez

Bibliographic information published by the German National Library:

The German National Library lists this publication in the National Bibliography; detailed bibliographic data are available on the Internet at http://dnb.dnb.de.

ISBN: 9783346389985
This book is also available as an ebook.

© GRIN Publishing GmbH
Nymphenburger Straße 86
80636 München

Print and binding: Books on Demand GmbH, Norderstedt, Germany
Printed on acid-free paper from responsible sources.

The present work has been carefully prepared. Nevertheless, authors and publishers do not incur liability for the correctness of information, notes, links and advice as well as any printing errors.

GRIN web shop: https://www.grin.com/document/1005942

Project Summary

Public engagement in environmental and public safety decisions are critical in maintaining and preserving National and State parks. Maintaining regulations regarding safety practices of active nuclear power plants and decommissioning power plants are necessary for the safety of nearby communities, protection of surrounding wildlife and the prevention of a major nuclear accident. As fossil fuels are a known major contributor to climate change, the use of nuclear power around the world, and in the United States, is a topic of controversy. Nuclear power in the U.S. accounts for <u>more than 30%</u> of the world's nuclear generated electricity (World Nuclear Association, 2019). Citizens and policy makers often dispute whether nuclear power is, or could be in the future, a sufficient alternative to fossil fuels.

Less understood by the public is the issue of what can be done with nuclear waste generated from nuclear power plants. It is often misconstrued that those advocating for safe disposal and transportation of nuclear waste are against nuclear power, which is another issue, yet not separate from the topic of nuclear waste disposal.

The San Onofre State Beach Park in San Onofre, California is the home of the decommissioned San Onofre Nuclear Generating Station (SONGS) and the Independent Spent Fuel Storage Installation (ISFSI) where nuclear waste is being "temporarily" stored. The corporation in charge of both sites, Southern California Edison, has obscured and intentionally concealed important facts regarding public safety.

The public has the right to know what is happening at the sites because it is a critical matter of public safety. The public cannot push for policy change on behalf of the safety of those nearby and the environment without an understanding of what Southern California Edison is actually doing with the nuclear waste. Public Watchdogs of San Diego is working diligently to accomplish two things; to expose the truth of what is happening at the San Onofre State Beach Park and to stop the completion of a substandard 'temporary' storage solution that could potentially endanger all life in Southern California. The devastating repercussions of a nuclear accident at the San Onofre State Beach Park could last for thousands of years.

I have been tasked with the responsibility of helping to create insights and story angles from June 3, 2019 until October 24, 2019 over 40 hours per week to bring attention to the issue of nuclear waste at San Onofre. Part of the objective of Public Watchdogs is public and environmental advocacy by summoning public will, which I learned about from reading Pezullo's, *"Environmental Communication and the Public Sphere."* Public will is the desire of many people for change that evidently pushes policy makers to make these changes. The complex findings from my research on the issue were translated into simple and engaging story angles for the public. Many creative presentations of story angles were released to the public, and some are yet to be released, in support of the legal filings by Public Watchdogs to stop the burial of nuclear waste at San Onofre and to enforce stricter safety standards. A significant and recent challenge to my work is that all content must be cleared by a former TV news anchor and a legal team. This created additional communication challenges and learning opportunities.

Table of Contents

1. Introduction

I was told about Public Watchdogs in September of 2018 by a previous employer, who is now a frequent donor to the 501 © nonprofit. On August 9, 2018, a "whistleblower" employed by a Southern California Edison (SCE) contractor by the name of David Fritch spoke out at a public hearing sponsored by Edison exposing the truth of the August 3, 2018 "near-miss" accident that occurred on site. A thin-walled stainless-steel canister of nuclear waste suspended in the air fell nearly 18 feet without a "canister enclosure cavity." If the canister had broken, radiation would have been released into the atmosphere, and the severity of the potential consequences are unknown. SCE failed to report this incident to the Nuclear Regulatory Commission (NRC), as required by law. This incident was a pressing issue when I returned home to San Diego for winter break, and I became interested in learning more.

I became substantively engaged with the issue when I found out that everyone in San Diego and Orange County was in immediate danger of radioactive nuclear waste. I learned that my entire hometown could face irreparable destruction, and become uninhabitable. Most people in San Diego and Orange County were completely unaware. My first reaction was to believe that the government would never allow something like this to happen in the United States, let alone in my hometown. I was shocked to find out that government organizations are partially responsible for this immense danger in Southern California. If a major nuclear accident were to occur in Southern California, the area could be uninhabitable for thousands of years. I thought that if a major accident were to occur while I was away in Miami, I would have no home which to return. The possibility of mass evacuations and fears of radiation induced illness filled my mind. However, the issue is *far* larger than the permanent evacuation of my childhood home. It involves public safety of local communities, potential toxic contamination of the entire Pacific Ocean, the destruction of habitats, loss of multiple species from the face of the earth and the loss of sacred historical land. Moreover, the issue also involves the future of nuclear waste disposal practices of decommissioned plants across the United States. I found out that Public Watchdogs is the only organization legally challenging the organizations who are responsible for putting Southern California in nuclear danger.

Every time I thought I understood the complexity of the issue at San Onofre, I discovered a new element of the problem and an entirely new angle of the story unfolded. I recognized the need for this complex issue to be broken down into something the public could easily grasp. At first I believed that the multiplicity of pieces to the story was a burden or a potential weakness because it was difficult to transform this topic into something the public would be able to learn about quickly; but now I recognize each angle as a different hook that could be used and I was able to engage a greater number of citizens. I learned that the depth and complexity of the issue could be used as a benefit.

1.1 Background

San Onofre State Beach Park is the birthplace of surf culture in Southern California. It is home to the famous surf breaks; Trestles and Church. It is home to an array of terrestrial and marine wildlife. It was also once the ancestral home and ancient burial ground of the Acjachemen Tribal Nation who claim to have lived at San Onofre for at least 10,000 years.

Today, 3.6 million pounds of nuclear waste sits in 'temporary storage' on the site either underwater in the spent fuel pools where the nuclear waste is stored or in the storage canisters. The storage canisters encase the nuclear waste in 5/8" thick stainless steel, protected by only 15 feet of seawall, 108 feet away from the beach. The canisters were not built to withstand salt air, and they are only guaranteed to last for a mere 25 years. The nuclear waste will remain deadly for thousands of years. This storage system is only meant to be a 'temporary' storage solution until another location for the nuclear waste to be transported to is found. However, Public Watchdogs uncovered that the legal definition of 'temporary' could actually mean up to 300 years. As of today, 34 of the 73 nuclear waste canisters have been buried in the Independent Spent Fuel Storage Installation (ISFSI) in carbon steel storage silos inside of earthen beams. Once buried, the canisters cannot be retrieved from the ground, so they will not be able to be transported anywhere without cracking (Public Watchdogs, 2019). The canisters are already estimated to be damaged, but there is no way to check once they are buried (San Onofre Safety, 2019). Once the canisters become cracked, there is no safe method to repair them underground and the release of deadly radioactive waste cannot be stopped (San Onofre Safety, 2019). The nuclear waste that has not been buried remains in the spent fuel pools.

When the radiation levels of the spent fuel pools get too high, SCE dumps the contaminated radioactive waste water into the Pacific Ocean under the procedure, 'Dilute and Discharge.' As radiation is nearly impossible to detect in water, the impact of this practice is unknown. However, to compensate for the damage that was found by the California Coastal Commission, SCE was court-ordered to fund the creation of Wheeler North Reef, the largest artificial reef in the United States. Wheeler North Reef has yet to be deemed a 'successful' reef. One of the measurements of success required by the California Coastal Commission is by the amount of fish it attracts. The Coastal Commission has required Wheeler North Reef to acquire a minimum biomass of 28 tons of fish (Reed and Shroeter, 2017). Wheeler North Reef has failed to meet that requirement every year (Reed and Shroeter, 2017). Instead of focusing on fostering a hospitable environment for marine life within the area, SCE is currently using taxpayer money to pay for the expansion of the reef in order to meet minimum requirements. Even though the plant is no longer running, the 'once-through cooling' system is still active, drawing in 42 million gallons of water daily and returning the water about 19 degrees Fahrenheit warmer to the Pacific Ocean (Reed and Shroeter, 2017). Expanding the reef around this "thermal plume," the area that is being heated by the once-through cooling process, might give the reef a better chance at finally meeting this requirement although damage is still being caused (San Onofre Safety, 2019).

The nuclear waste site at San Onofre is a public health threat to 8.5 million Southern California residents living within the 50-mile plume zone, which is the area identified by the Nuclear Regulatory Commission (NRC) that is subject to risk of radiation (Public Watchdogs, 2019). The exact consequences of radiation being released from San Onofre are dependent upon the amount of radiation that is released as well as other factors such as whether or not the accident happens in the spent fuel pools or underground.

Once all of the nuclear waste at SONGS is buried, current law dictates that it is no longer the responsibility of SCE, and it will become the public's responsibility. Burying the nuclear waste on site at San Onofre is the cheapest, and fastest solution for SCE. Transporting it elsewhere has been discussed, but there is no legal alternative place to transport it to, and it is suspected that the thin-walled nuclear waste canisters could crack during the journey (San Onofre Safety, 2019). A site was under construction at Yucca Mountain, Nevada but the state of Nevada has refused to allow Yucca Mountain to accept the waste, and the indigenous people who live nearby did not want to take on the burden and danger of hosting the nuclear waste.

On August 30, 2019, Public Watchdogs called for court intervention to stop the burial of nuclear waste at San Onofre because neither the canisters nor the decommissioning plan have undergone a proper safety assessment. The canisters are buried 108 feet from the water, in a tsunami inundation zone, near the Newport Inglewood earthquake fault, and on a bluff threatened by erosion. New research shows Newport Inglewood is as deep and as potentially deadly as the San Andreas fault. The NRC, which is in charge of the decommissioning oversight, has not enforced effective safety practices. When SCE failed to disclose the 'near-miss' incident on August 3, 2018, this was a violation of federal law. The NRC issued SCE a $116,000.00 fine, which is virtually irrelevant given SCE's hundreds of millions of dollars in annual profits. Public Watchdogs is advocating for safer management of the nuclear waste, and has initiated multiple legal actions to stop the unsafe burial process.

1.2 Project Proposal

The purpose of this internship project was to provide Public Watchdogs with communication strategies and outputs that effectively supported the goal of creating awareness and understanding among the general public of the complex issues. In addition, this project was to engage the public in pushing for policy change and safer regulations. All strategies and executions were supported by communication theories and studies that are relevant to environmental policy and public advocacy.

I proposed to (1) spread general awareness and understanding about the nuclear waste issue at San Onofre; (2) to encourage the Public Watchdogs primary target audience, identified by Charles Langley, the Executive Director, to donate financial resources to help the cause; (3) and to promote the Public Watchdogs petition to "[revoke] California permits allowing the unsafe burial of nuclear waste."

To execute these objectives, I proposed to strategically create messages to the public that were framed to convey the complexity of the issue regarding the dumping of nuclear waste so they could understand the crucial components of the issue. All of the messages were to be based on research. From there, the goal was to get the public to sign a Public Watchdogs petition that called on government intervention to stop the burial process at San Onofre after successfully informing them on the issue. It was anticipated that the power of the public opinion would influence the policy makers.

1.3 Project Outcome

I completed the research, and created unique and creative messages in congruence with the original goals for the internship, which were to spread general awareness and encourage the public to influence policy change. However, the information was actually utilized for a purpose other than to get the public to make an informed decision to sign the Public Watchdogs' petition. Instead of using the research and creative methods to promote the petition, the content was used to support the Public Watchdogs legal filings. It was determined that the research and ensuing information was too critical and that it would be best utilized in a court venue. It remained my goal to keep the public engaged with the legal filings. Content was frequently posted to the Public Watchdogs' website and Facebook page. I also participated in public hearings regarding the nuclear waste issue. I spoke at public hearings as well as networked, and kept in contact with attendees. To keep the public engaged and interested in following Public Watchdogs' legal efforts, I continued to create content examining the issues from different angles.

1.4 Purpose and Significance of Project

The purpose of this project was to develop a series of story angles and outputs that reach the public and spread general awareness by using framing. In the process, scientific arguments and incriminating evidence derived from research were linked to human emotion in such a way that put the issue of nuclear waste at San Onofre into perspective for the public. The approach was similar to the SANE ads in 1962 of the notorious Dr. Spock that "warned of the risks to people and the nonhuman world in ecological systems increasingly burdened by pollution, toxicity, and other hazards" (Dunaway, 2015). The Dr. Spock ad was meant to change the public perception of nuclear bomb testing in 1962 to something "ominous," which was something I kept in mind while expressing each story angle (Dunaway, 2015). Each story angle was created with the intent to provoke a feeling of an immediate threat. The goal was to frame the story angle in such a way that made the issue a concern to the individual viewer. Since people often resort to the media to interpret environmental issues, it was appropriate to focus on using social media to break down the issue of nuclear waste at San Onofre from various frames. I used the concept of Shome and Marx's "mental models" to present environmental news in such a way that aligned with viewers and allowed them to adopt the position that the information source took (Shome and Marx, 2009). For example, I avoided the use of framing the issue from the perspective of any political party as not to conflict with any viewer's preexisting beliefs. Framing was used in this project often to create and reconstruct these mental models of various viewers.

2. Description of Project

The analysis of Public Watchdogs' "social media network" was attempted in this project in order to create different frames, and to reach a wider range of people in the Southern California community (Fine and Kanter, 2010). While analyzing Public Watchdogs' complex social media network, I found certain "hubs" that helped us connect to "nodes" that existed more on the "edge of periphery" (Fine and Kanter, 2010). For example, as will be explained in further detail in the "Materials" section, I discovered that Adelia Sandoval, a spiritual spokesperson for the Acjachemen Nation, is a "hub" with multiple connections to other nearby indigenous communities. While working with her, and helping her to communicate the nuclear waste issue from an Acjachemen member's perspective, I was able to strengthen the "tie" between Public Watchdogs and the Acjachemen, and I am hopeful this will encourage involvement from nearby indigenous communities on the "edge of [our] periphery" once the Acjachemen story is posted on our website (Fine and Kanter, 2010).

2.1 Objectives

Multiple different story angles were identified and expanded upon, and each of them had a specific function within the big picture of the issue. Each story angle is later described in the "Materials" section. The objective of each identified story angle was to create content that would get the public engaged and help them achieve a fuller understanding of the issue.

With complex issues such as the one at San Onofre, the public often only receives exposure to bits and pieces of the information on the topic, leading to an insufficient understanding of the problem as a whole. When this happens, perceptions around who is to blame and what should be done are often misconstrued.

As the public attention span towards content on the internet is limited and often times difficult to obtain, the objective was to introduce pieces to the puzzle over an extended period of time that could each stand on their own without generating misconceptions. As it is nearly impossible to capture the public's attention long enough for them to learn everything there is to know about the nuclear waste issue in one sitting, I realized that a full understanding of the issue was something that must be acquired over time. For example, the problems with where and how the waste is buried are one piece of the issue. However, the once-through cooling system that is being used for the canisters that have not been buried is another issue because the process is hurting marine life in the area. This is why many who are unaware of the environmental impacts of burying the canisters, but are aware of the problems at Wheeler North Reef, believe that the burial process should happen faster. Each piece of the puzzle is interesting on its own, but one cannot make an informed decision without understanding the complexity of the problem. I used Cox and Hansen's concepts of "niche topics" to create story angles that present this "environmental beat" issue in such a way that is competitive enough to capture the public attention (Cox and Hansen, 2015).

The big-picture focus was to introduce the public to the Public Watchdogs' lawsuit filed in order to stop the burial of nuclear waste, and to generate awareness regarding why the nuclear waste burial process should be stopped in order to enforce public safety. All of the content that was created for each angle became information that supplemented the lawsuit. Much of the social media content links to the Public Watchdogs site where a copy of the <u>lawsuit</u> and <u>Temporary Restraining Order</u> can be found (Public Watchdogs, 2019).

2.2 Project Results

Prior to starting my work at Public Watchdogs, Facebook posts tended to reach up to 20 engagements. The results of my project were successful, as I created content that engaged multiple members of the public. On one occasion, I was able to successfully engage more than 30,000 people, and 1,700 people clicked through to the Public Watchdogs' website. This also happened to be the day after the filing of the Public Watchdogs' major lawsuit, so engagement was critical during this time.

Public Watchdogs was also able to secure interviews with CBS Channel 8, ABC 10 News, and KUSI Channel 9 News regarding the lawsuit. All of the content that was shared with the public was required to have been cleared by the legal team. This made it especially challenging to post content in a timely manner. However, as a result, I also gained experience and helpful feedback from former TV news anchor, Lynn Stewart, on all of my content after August 28, 2019.

2.2.1 Methodology

Each story angle was created through extensive internet research, information provided at public hearings, or through the reviewing of legal documents. Multiple mediums were used to create engaging content, such as, Hootsuite, Canva, Facebook, MailChimp, Google Maps, and Microsoft Word. I used Hootsuite to organize and schedule my social media posts.

(Photo of typical Hootsuite schedule)

I used Canva to create visual memos, often to supplement text.

OCT 17, 2019

Coastal Commission VOTE on the San Onofre Nuclear Waste Dump

CHULA VISTA CITY HALL

9:00 AM

(Photo of an image I created using Canva for a Facebook post)

Facebook was the main form of social media used because the majority of Public Watchdogs target audience uses Facebook frequently. Examples of Facebook posts will be shown in the "Materials" section. MailChimp was used to organize important contacts, send newsletters to people with connections to TV media, and to those who had signed up to receive emailed information from Public Watchdogs.

(Example of Mail Chimp newsletter below)

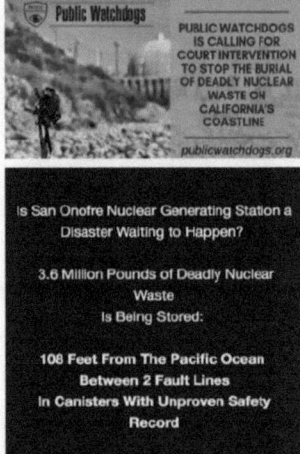

Public Watchdogs

Live Appearances and Interviews Available
Upon Request

Find Out More

I used Google Maps to create an interactive map that will be explained later in the "Materials" section. Microsoft Word was used to type blog posts, social media posts and other written content. For photo content, I created a list of possible story titles along with a photo 'wish list' of descriptions of photos I would like to have for upcoming posts. From there, I got a professional photographer to capture the photos described in my wish list.

(One of the photos captured from the wish list)

2.2.2 Materials

Story Angle 1: The nuclear waste disposal at SONGS as a public health and safety threat

The nuclear waste issue at San Onofre is a threat to the health and safety of those in Southern California in multiple different ways. I created an infographic illustrating key details of the issue as a public health threat. There are two different versions. One is a shorter version meant for social media and the other is a more detailed version that was meant to supplement the information surrounding the lawsuit on the Public Watchdogs' website, and for use as printed collateral at public events. This frame in particular was interesting to create with reference to Pearson's article on the relation between demographic representation and risk perception of climate change and environmental issues (Pearson, 2017). It was noted in this article that "environmental interventions" that involve government restrictions and encroach upon individual rights are often seen as a threat to conservatives, especially white males, whereas "regulations that emphasize collective rights and protection of minority populations often resonate with liberals" (Pearson, 2017). One of my goals was to depoliticize the issue altogether by framing this health threat as a problem that concerns everyone. When constructing this frame, I kept this article in close consideration in order to avoid negatively provoking either political party by focusing on the immediate dangers.

(Infographic example with more words for Public Watchdogs website under copies of the lawsuit and Temporary Restraining Order)

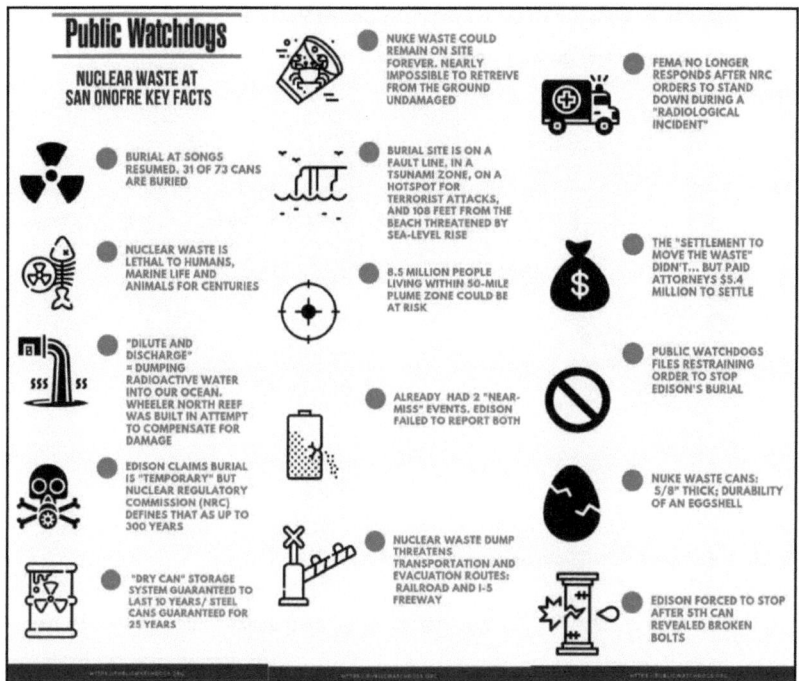

Public Watchdogs

NUCLEAR WASTE AT SAN ONOFRE KEY FACTS

NUKE WASTE COULD REMAIN ON SITE FOREVER. NEARLY IMPOSSIBLE TO RETREIVE FROM THE GROUND UNDAMAGED

FEMA NO LONGER RESPONDS AFTER NRC ORDERS TO STAND DOWN DURING A "RADIOLOGICAL INCIDENT"

BURIAL AT SONGS RESUMED, 31 OF 73 CANS ARE BURIED

BURIAL SITE IS ON A FAULT LINE, IN A TSUNAMI ZONE, ON A HOTSPOT FOR TERRORIST ATTACKS, AND 108 FEET FROM THE BEACH THREATENED BY SEA-LEVEL RISE

NUCLEAR WASTE IS LETHAL TO HUMANS, MARINE LIFE AND ANIMALS FOR CENTURIES

THE "SETTLEMENT TO MOVE THE WASTE" DIDN'T... BUT PAID ATTORNEYS $5.4 MILLION TO SETTLE

8.5 MILLION PEOPLE LIVING WITHIN 50-MILE PLUME ZONE COULD BE AT RISK

"DILUTE AND DISCHARGE" = DUMPING RADIOACTIVE WATER INTO OUR OCEAN. WHEELER NORTH REEF WAS BUILT IN ATTEMPT TO COMPENSATE FOR DAMAGE

PUBLIC WATCHDOGS FILES RESTRAINING ORDER TO STOP EDISON'S BURIAL

ALREADY HAD 2 "NEAR-MISS" EVENTS. EDISON FAILED TO REPORT BOTH

EDISON CLAIMS BURIAL IS "TEMPORARY" BUT NUCLEAR REGULATORY COMMISSION (NRC) DEFINES THAT AS UP TO 300 YEARS

NUKE WASTE CANS: 5/8" THICK; DURABILITY OF AN EGGSHELL

NUCLEAR WASTE DUMP THREATENS TRANSPORTATION AND EVACUATION ROUTES: RAILROAD AND I-5 FREEWAY

"DRY CAN" STORAGE SYSTEM GUARANTEED TO LAST 10 YEARS/ STEEL CANS GUARANTEED FOR 25 YEARS

EDISON FORCED TO STOP AFTER 5TH CAN REVEALED BROKEN BOLTS

(Infographic example with less words for social media)

Story Angle 2: Southern California Edison as setting the national precedent

Decommissioning, and soon-to-be-decommissioned power plants around the nation are watching to see what SCE is going to be able to get away with at San Onofre. The argument here is that this is not merely a local issue. It is actually in everyone's 'backyard.' The interactive map I created allows people to click through each icon and see the name of each power plant in the country; it has a photo of the power plant so that many people will recognize the plant closest to them; it includes the name of the congress member in charge of the plant with the contact information of the corresponding congress member; and the activity status of the plant and the decommissioning date if applicable. The goal of the interactive map was to get people to contact their local congress members to express their safety concerns regarding the plants, and to help people understand that no matter where we are in the United States, we are not far from a power plant. Many of us have nuclear power plants in our hometowns.

(Photo of interactive map)

Story Angle 3: Compare SONGS circumstances to Fukushima

The Fukushima disaster in 2011 was started by an earthquake, followed by a tsunami, followed by the nuclear accident. Because Fukushima was an event that so many people have heard of, and fear, it was a good reference to compare to the situation at San Onofre. I came up with a few shocking findings worth sharing with the public after conducting extensive research. For example, the seawall protecting Fukushima Daiichi was 42 feet high while the seawall at San Onofre, the only thing that stands between the ISFISI burial site and the beach, is only 15 feet high. I also discovered that there is a fault directly under the nuclear waste site. SCE has hired multiple seismologists to look for this fault, but all of them have 'looked' everywhere except where the fault is actually located. Seismologists who have not been funded by SCE have identified the fault, and it is named the Oceanside Blind Thrust. Blind thrusts are not usually the most powerful types of earthquake faults but they can be particularly destructive. Unfortunately, I could not include this information in the blog post because it interfered with the current legal filings, but I look forward to sharing this information with the public in the future. I wrote a blog post for this topic linking Public Watchdogs' efforts to the California Earthquake Authority (CEA). The post was about preparing Southern California for an event like Fukushima.

Story Angle 4: (Dilute and Discharge) the untold story of Wheeler North Reef

The California Coastal Commission (CCC) ordered Southern California Edison (SCE) to compensate for the damage caused to the nearby marine habitat while SONGS was an active plant. 2.4 billion gallons of water were taken from the ocean and transported to SONGS to cool down the plant. The process is called once-through cooling. The corporation was charged with the responsibility of building an artificial reef that meets the requirement that the artificial reef must attract a minimum of 28 tons of fish biomass. SCE has yet to meet this requirement, and is in the process of requesting to expand the artificial reef in order to meet this requirement using taxpayer money. Wheeler North Reef is already one of the world's largest reefs. The inactive plant continues to actively harm the marine life and pollute the water nearby.

Now that the plant is decommissioned, SONGS still takes 42 million gallons of seawater daily, and it is unknown what it is being used for, but I suspect it is used in the practice called 'Dilute and Discharge' where contaminated water from the spent fuel pools at SONGS is diluted with more seawater, and then released back into the Pacific Ocean about 19 degrees warmer than when it was taken (Reed and Shroeter, 2017).

I decided to present this story angle in a blog post, highlighting the most important facts I found through the multiple pages of scientific reports and legal filings I reviewed, and the public hearings I attended. The public should not have to sift through endless pages of documents to find this information. The intention of the blog post was to make this information regarding the full story behind the spent fuel pools easier and faster for the public to access.

One of my arguments with this story angle was that the reef will not be habitable for marine life if Edison continues to 'Dilute and Discharge' contaminated wastewater into the marine habitat. Expanding the reef in order to meet the minimum requirement of fish only masks the harm done to the marine life by polluting the area with radioactive waste water. When counting the area around the part of the reef that is being heated by the 'Dilute and Discharge' water, it will be easier to meet the requirements set by the California Coastal Commission (CCC) because the reef will extend outside of the thermal plume.

Another argument I make is that the public is not informed when SCE discharges polluted water into the reef, but they should be. The Wheeler North Reef is a popular recreational dive site, and the public has the right to know when and where this contaminated water is being discharged. My goal of exposing this information is to push Southern California Edison to begin notifying the public when they discharge radioactive water by gathering "public will" to change the policy (Cox and Pezullo).

According to Cox and Hansen, "...energy sometimes draws high levels of interest when politicians are blaming one another for high gas prices, or an oil company dumps a million gallons of crude oil into the Gulf of Mexico" (Cox and Hansen, 2015). I used these ideas as inspiration for creating the story angle for Wheeler North Reef, which emphasizes the fact that taxpayer money was being used to expand the artificial reef that Edison has been ordered to create, and that radioactive waste water is being 'Diluted and discharged' into the Pacific Ocean right off the coast of San Onofre.

After being transparent about the risks and current harm caused by the operation of the spent fuel pools, I then explain why destroying the spent fuel pools and moving forward with the alternative is an even larger threat to the environment. I make it clear that it is not that Public Watchdogs does not agree that the spent fuels are dangerous, but the alternative of taking the nuclear waste out of the spent fuel pools and burying it in the current containers at the current location poses a larger risk, and may cause even more damage to the environment in the future. The spent fuel pools are also the only safety precaution in place if a nuclear release were to happen with one of the canisters, so destroying the pools before completing the burial process seems irresponsible. I supplemented this article by voicing my argument at the California Coastal Commission public hearing on October 17, 2019. Unfortunately, the Coastal Commission unanimously voted to have the spent fuel pools destroyed and to move forward with the burial process.

Story Angle 5: The ancient burial ground; words from the rightful owners of the land

I discovered that SONGS was built upon an ancient Acjachemen burial site. I conducted an interview with Adelia Sandoval, the Acjachemen spiritual leader, to get her insight on what was happening at SONGS to create a blog post.

The Acjachemen were not displaced by SONGS, as they were initially displaced by Spanish invaders who renamed them the 'Juaneno Band of Mission Indians.' Through extensive preliminary research, I found that an engineer in charge of the construction of SONGS found the remains of three different bodies that were identified as Acjachemen. Instead of reporting the finding to the police and stopping the construction process, the man took the remains and hid them in his house (Public Watchdogs, 2019). Upon his death, his family sent the remains in the mail to the Acjachemen Tribal Nation (Public Watchdogs, 2019).

The Acjachemen have struggled to regain their identity after being renamed and displaced by the Spanish, and to this day, people still at times reference them as 'Juaneno.' The Acjachemen are active advocates for safer management practices in the nuclear waste issue at San Onofre. Although they no longer live on that part of the land, they still see themselves as stewards of the San Onofre State Beach Park even though they are not federally recognized as a nation entitled to that area. SONGS is not just on a State Beach Park, it is on historic, sacred, land that holds immense value to a reviving culture.

Adelia Sandoval's insight was profound, and the public should have exposure to the nuclear waste issue from an Acjachemen representative's perspective. Part of the nuclear waste issue involves environmental racism in the sense that some of the public is pushing to have the nuclear waste imparted onto an indigenous community in Yucca Valley, California and away from the 8.5 million people who live near San Onofre. Many who are aware of the environmental racism in moving the waste to Yucca Valley are advocating to keep the waste where it is in San Onofre. Most people don't know, however, that the site at San Onofre is also on sacred indigenous land, and keeping it here is also threatening an indigenous culture. I found that most people in San Diego don't even know who the Acjachemen are. This is why I thought it was so important to create a story angle for the Acjachemen Nation. Not only would it help shed light on what's happening at San Onofre, but it will also make viewers aware of the Acjachemen

Nation. This story angle is intended to reduce the number of advocates for unsafe permanent storage at San Onofre because it is on a reviving indigenous culture's sacred land.

less inclined to advocate for unsafe permanent storage on an indigenous culture's sacred land.

Story Angle 6: The issue of nuclear waste from the perspective of younger generations (memes)

Throughout my internship, I have struggled to engage younger generations on the issue, especially on Facebook. Many prefer to avoid environmental politics, even if they consider themselves 'environmentalists,' and prefer to use Facebook primarily for entertainment. I came up with the idea to bridge the gap between the attention of younger generations and this complex, environmental, political issue by creating a series of entertaining 'memes.' All of the memes were intended to link to a landing page on the Public Watchdogs' site where people can learn more about the nuclear waste issue at San Onofre. These memes and landing pages will not be posted until after the Judge has ruled on the lawsuit because the legal team has advised us not to post any informal content that might generate the perception that Public Watchdogs is an 'activist' organization, and not a 'public advocacy' organization. If we are seen as 'activists,' the Judge might be more inclined to disregard our legal filings. I intend to frame the issue in such a way that emphasizes the fact that the issue of nuclear waste at San Onofre is especially a concern to future generations. It is an issue that is an immediate threat to public safety and the environment, if the waste were to be left where it is at San Onofre. It will likely become a problem for future generations to have to manage. The memes I created are intentionally informal. I anticipate that the memes will be very successful once they are posted when the legal oversight on Public Watchdogs social media activity lessens.

(Some of the memes)

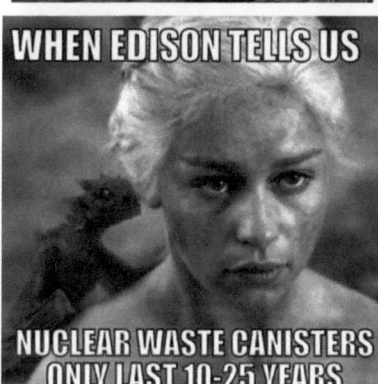

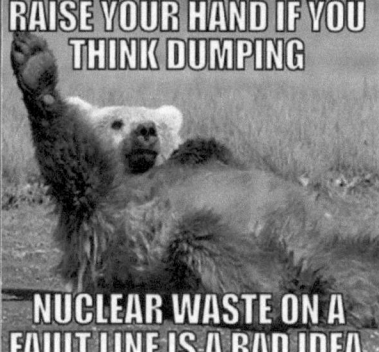

DUMPS SO DEADLY

EVERYONE WITHIN 50 MILES WILL FEEL IT.

Other Work: Challenge Coins, Merchandise, Newspaper Wrap, Social Media, Public Hearings

Challenge Coins:

San Diego is a military town with major Naval and Marine bases. Commemorative coins, known as "challenge coins," are given to military members as part of a symbol for an achievement, and they are highly valued and collected. Because there are so many San Diego and Orange County residents affiliated with the military, I thought it would be a good idea to thank

24

donors by sending them a Public Watchdogs' challenge coin, something military families would find familiar and appreciate. Attached to the following page is my rough design for the challenge coins that will be sent to a professional designer to create.

(Challenge coin design side A)

(Challenge coin design side B)

Merchandise:

The merchandise is an attempt to members of the community outside of the usual target of older locals with the time and money to spend on the issue. In one of the ECS 612 Readings, *Research in Human Ecology*, it talks about a study that examines consumer behavior that tests the theory that as consumer values change, their purchasing behavior will not. One of the big-picture ideas of this study is that, in order to "mobilize support," activists should link the cause to something that the target values, frame the current state of the situation as a threat to those values, and then bring awareness to the targets' power to reverse this threat. I thought it would be wise to create something that could mobilize support within San Onofre surf culture because one of the most popular surf spots in California is located right in front of the plant Since San Onofre is a major hotspot for surfers, I thought it would be wise to create something that could coexist with the San Onofre surf culture. This is challenging considering surfers can tend to "tune out" when they hear that their favorite surf spots, Trestles and Church, might not be safe to surf anymore. All of the merchandise I designed is meant to be symbolic of the issue, but still manifest as something people can identify with enough to wear on display. The angle I chose for reaching this segment was to make something "cool" that aligns with San Onofre surf culture, and to avoid using the public health frame I used for Story Angle 1. Instead, the focus was on locals being against a corporation for polluting a well- renowned surf spot. Through research, and growing up in Southern California, I learned that San Onofre surf culture tends to embody a heavy sense of localism. My goal was to redirect the San Onofre surf culture's territorial tendency towards Southern California Edison. This merchandise has not been created yet, but my intention was for Public Watchdogs to sponsor surfing events at San Onofre and sell this merchandise there. Even with the knowledge of what is happening at San Onofre, I have found that passionate surfers are more likely to support safer packaging of the waste than to actually get out of the water that might be exposing them to radiation. So instead of encouraging them to get out of the water, which likely will not happen, the goal was to get them involved in stopping SCE from polluting 'their' beach. The point of making merchandise was to create something people can identify with enough to keep it out on display, spreading awareness to anyone they come in contact with.

(Examples of merchandise designs)

(Images on the t-shirts will be scaled larger and the white background will be removed in the final design)

(Examples of Iphone case merchandise designs)

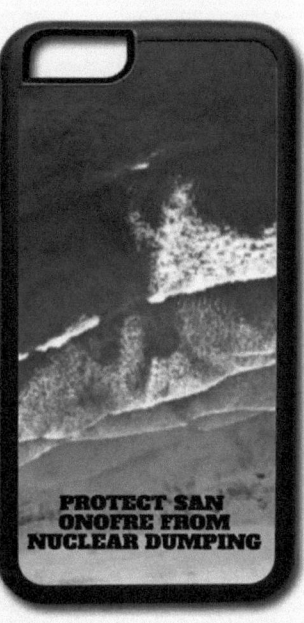

(Design for pet bandana)

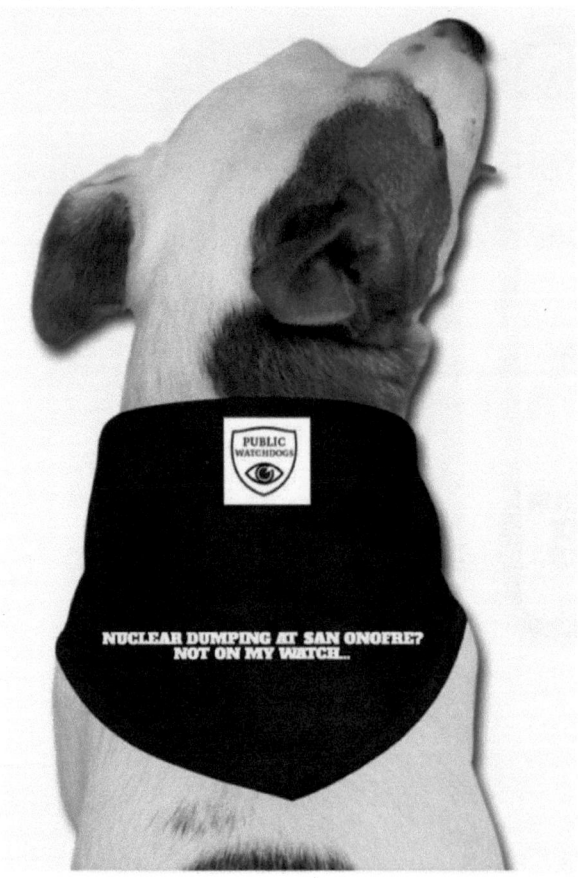

(Women's crop top design)

Newspaper Wrap:

I was asked to create a mock-up design of a newspaper wrap during this internship. I was also given the task of getting the prices and availability for the San Diego Union Tribune, Los Angeles Times, and the Orange County Register. The ideal scenario was to air a Public Watchdogs public service announcement on Sunday morning in congruence with the newspaper wrap in all three newspapers to coastal zip codes in San Diego and Orange County. There were multiple different sizes to consider for the newspaper wraps, all of which had different pricing. When purchased in packages, pricing changes. Pricing also changes if you are a nonprofit, if you buy more than one spot, and depending on whether the ads are black and white, or 4-color (full-color), and the type of material used. This task proved to be rather challenging as I had no prior experience with media purchasing, and I had little experience with printed newspapers in general. I attended an Excel seminar to improve my Excel skills to learn to create an extensive pricing guide for one of the funders of Public Watchdogs to review. I also attended a meeting with a representative from the San Diego Union Tribune to discuss pricing, details, and next steps for the newspaper wrap. The pricing guide on Excel is finished, and will be used as an internal reference for Public Watchdogs. Moving forward with the wrap has been postponed until after the legal actions lessen, but I have mapped out some content and design ideas for the newspaper outlets to reference when they create the final wrap.

(Newspaper wrap mock-up design side B)

(Note that side B is not completely filled out to leave room for announcing the anticipated legal filings)

The settlement to move the waste didn't

San Clemente, the official location of San Onofre, has the most stranded nuclear waste in the country.

To put in perspective just how much waste San Clemente has, only 13 pounds of plutonium killed 80,000 people in Nagasaki. There is 3.6 million pounds of nuclear waste sitting at Son Onofre.

SCE claims that the storage system they are using is only a "temporary" solution. The federal definition of "temporary" could imply up to 300 years. The canisters may barely last for 30 years.

SCE has already had two accidents that almost ravaged all of Southern California.

The NRC refers to these accidents as "near-hits." The reason that these "near-hits" are public knowledge is because a courageous San Onofre Safety Officer exposed the truth of these events during a public meeting.

There was once a lawsuit called, the "Settlement to move the waste," but the settlement did not actually move the waste anywhere.

The law firm was paid $5 million to abandon the case.

The closure of this settlement has costed rate payers an unsettling amount as a result of SCE's publicly funded failed nuclear reactors.

It costed an estimate of $4.7 billion to close the power plant, $3.3 billion for rate payers to bail Edison out after the closure instead of Edison stockholders, $775 million for the settlement amount that shaved off $3.3 billion customers not to pay in the future, and $2.525 billion in remaining closing costs that customers will pay instead of Edison stockholders.

The settlement was decided in secret without any public hearings.

Public Watchdogs filed formal comments in the form of a legal protest on a proposed decision to bail out SCE for its failed nuclear reactors.

Public Watchdog's iconic HazMat surfer warns San Onofre of the dangers they face. High levels of radiation may be present in the ocean near the nuclear waste site. The dangers will only get worse if SCE successfully buries the nuclear waste.

What's happening with the radioactive waste right now?

The 50 sirens that were to be used to alert the community of an emergency will be taken down Monday, July 1.

This week, there has been suspicion that SCE has already resumed burying the nuclear waste before a public hearing or authorization from the NRC.

The 30" canister was prepared to be buried before SCE was asked to stop the burial process, so once SCE resumes, they could have the 30" canister buried in less than a day.

THE TOXIC TRUTH ABOUT SAN ONOFRE

Southern California Edison (SCE) puts 8.5 million lives in danger, burying 3.6 tons of nuclear waste 108 feet from the San Onofre State Beach

(Newspaper wrap side A)

Will San Onofre be the site of the next nuclear disaster?

The Nuclear Regulatory Commission (NRC) has refused to fine Holtec, the company responsible for creating SCE's canisters that hold nuclear waste, for redesigning them without complying with the required safety check.

The new canisters do not have the safety features that were there during the most recent safety check.

Charles Langley, the executive director of the Public Watchdogs, said Tuesday, June 25, 2019, "The way that the NRC has allowed Edison to manage the nuclear waste is irresponsible. This is likely the largest threat to public safety in the United States."

The NRC claims they are "protecting people and the environment," yet they have failed to do so.

The canisters were redesigned to be more economical for SCE at the expense of the safety of the tax payers who live near San Onofre State Park.

If you live within 50 miles of San Onofre, you are one of the 8.5 million people who reside within the plume zone if, and when, a nuclear disaster occurs at the site.

As of now, there are 73,100,000 pound canisters of lethal radioactive waste at the San Onofre State Park. Each thin-walled canister is only guaranteed to withstand for 10-25 years while the toxic waste they hold will be deadly for more than 250,000 years.

If the canisters do withstand for the estimated 10-25 years, there is still the risk of a major nuclear disaster that could happen at any time due to the location of the canisters.

This is not a future threat. Everyone who is within the 50-mile plume zone is in danger right now.

29 of the 73 canisters have already been buried near the Newport-Inglewood earthquake fault line. There is no evidence to support the assumption that the canisters can withstand an earthquake.

According to the NRC, who has repeated on multiple occasions, "The plant is safe, [and] the risk is low," but the danger at hand does not involve the decommissioned power plant.

The nuclear waste buried next to the site is what the public should be concerned about.

There is no data supporting the claim that "the risk is low." The risk of a major nuclear disaster at San Onofre is not low.

The burial site is 108 feet away from the beach, right in the middle of a tsunami zone, 3 feet away from the water table, it is in an area prone to a terrorist attack, and it is on a bluff threatened by corrosion and sea level rise.

Do something with this blank space

San Onofre's decommissioned Nuclear Generating Station is storing its radioactive nuclear waste on nearby sites on the beach. The waste will be lethal for more than 10,000 years.

What Southern California Edison doesn't want you to <u>know</u>

MADISON ALVAREZ

DATE

There will be no evacuation route because nuclear waste site is located right next to the I-5 freeway.

There is no emergency planning preparedness response because, in 2012, SCE applied for exemptions from emergency planning and the Nuclear Regulatory Commission (NRC) granted it.

As of now, the NRC no longer requires the Federal Management Agency (FEMA) to respond or report to the public in the case of an emergency at the site.

The Public Watchdogs, a local non-profit, has been keeping tabs on the NRC and SCE every step of their way to failure.

The NRC has repeatedly allowed SCE to keep mistakes that concern the public's safety a secret.

"The public has a right to know," said Nina Babiarz, board member of the Public Watchdogs.

For inside details about the secrets that the NRC and SCE don't want you to know, the Public watchdogs has posted the *Radiological Regulatory Failure* on their website. It explains all of the "near-hit" unsecured loading events that SCE has tried to hide from the public.

The Public Watchdogs of San Diego is keeping an eye on Southern California Edison, Holtec, and the Nuclear Regulatory Commission

The Public Watchdogs has currently filed a lawsuit against SCE, and other accomplices, who knowingly contributed to the storage of the nuclear waste, known as spent fuel, at the San Onofre Nuclear Generating Station (SONGS) without the legal right to do so.

This has put millions in danger.

The Public Watchdogs is also suing Holtec, the company responsible for designing the canisters that are currently storing the spent fuel, for making the walls 5/8 of an inch thick while standard industry canisters are 18-24 inches thick.

5/8 of an inch of steel is the only thing containing the nuclear waste from the environment. What will happen when the radioactive waste gets too hot within those canisters?

If the canisters were shrunk down to the size of an egg, the proportion of the canisters to the spent fuel inside would be similar to that of an egg shell.

The non-profit is demanding that the canisters of spent fuel that haven't been buried be put in safer containers, and for the burial of the remaining canisters to stop.

<u>Social Media Posts:</u>

In outputs I created for social media, information from Pearson's article was used to engage and unite both political parties over this issue. For example, I used the fact that Edison is attempting to get a permit that restricts public access to areas of San Onofre Beach in order to engage conservatives in Edison's plan to destroy the spent fuel pools at SONGS, which will be necessary to cool down overheated nuclear waste in the case of an emergency. The idea behind this was that conservatives would want to protect their right to access the public beaches. Then in another post, I attempted to engage liberals by promoting Public Watchdogs' legal actions to call on government intervention to protect the San Onofre State Beach Park from the potential radioactive pollution generated from the San Onofre Nuclear Generating Station (SONGS). However, I avoided tying the issue directly to partisanship as not to conflict with any preexisting beliefs viewers might associate with the posts.

Whenever there was an upcoming event, or relevant news story published, I would typically create a Word document with a list of multiple different post options to choose from. Charles and Nina would pick the best one, and I would then forward it to former TV anchor, Lynn Stewart, for edits from her and the legal team. Once she and the legal team approved a post, I would schedule it on Hootsuite to be posted for specific days and times depending on correspondence with upcoming events and popular times to post to social media.

On ABC10, Kimberly Hunt 10News interviews Public Watchdog's attorney Chuck LaBella, who says "we're not saying stop the decommissioning process. We're saying put the decommissioning process in perspective."

SDG&E has "no comment."

#publicwatchdogssd #SanOnofre #nuclearwaste #ABC10newsSD
https://bit.ly/2k6SHe8

YOUTUBE.COM
New legal action over nuclear waste at San Onofre Nuclear Generating Station

Public Watchdogs   •••
Published by Madison Alvarez [?] · August 30 at 1:41 PM · 🌐

This morning on CBS 8 - San Diego News Chris Gros covered Public
Watchdog's lawsuit to end the burial of nuclear waste #upwith8
#publicwatchdogssd #nuclearwaste #SONGS #SanOnofre

San Onofre Nuclear Emergency

https://www.cbs8.com/.../509-8e6e5932-b1c5-4be0-903c-315dcb65...

CBS8.COM
**Watchdog group calls for court to halt San Onofre nuclear
waste burial**

Public Hearings:

    I attended multiple public hearings on the nuclear waste issue at San Onofre. Three were in person and three were through webcam. I was provided an opportunity to represent future generations and participate during the public comments portion. I proposed questions to policy makers regarding whether or not sea-level rise has been considered in the design of the nuclear waste canisters. I asked policy makers to please consider future generations in their decision for temporary storage of the nuclear waste canisters. I also contributed to public comments by listing reasons why the California Coastal Commission should postpone their vote on a permit on October 17, 2019 that could potentially allow SCE to destroy the spent fuel cooling pools at San Onofre.

The public hearings that I attended in person were also an opportunity to network with other members of the community.

I am currently in the process of organizing with my former high school teacher and the Green Team Club at La Jolla Country Day High School to have the students join me in participating in the next public hearing. I plan to have each student speak during public comments at the next public hearing to show policy makers that future generations care about what is happening at San Onofre in the hope that they will be more inclined to considering future generations in their decision making process.

2.3 Analysis

I received substantial feedback on my work from the legal team, including former U.S. Attorney, Charles La Bella, the former TV news anchor who works with Public Watchdogs, Lynn Stewart, and Charles Langley and Nina Babiarz, board members of Public Watchdogs. Mostly positive feedback was given on my work. The issue of formality was occasionally discussed as it was often difficult for me to find a balance between creating engaging content versus content that does not generate the perception that Public Watchdogs is an 'activist' organization. Many informal images and text had to be censored. For example, Public Watchdogs owns the rights to a series of photos of a surfer in a "hazmat suit." The images are incredibly compelling and useful for getting the public's attention, but posting them on Facebook might give viewers the perception that we are informal protestors and not an advocacy group, so I was advised to refrain from using them until Public Watchdogs falls under less legal scrutiny. This limited the range of photos I could use on social media.

3. Discussion

Some tasks that were easy during this internship were creating the story angles, because the issue of nuclear waste at San Onofre naturally has multiple different sides of the story and has different people, and organizations involved. Creating different ways to introduce the subject was therefore not a challenge. It was also easy for me to generate engaging creative content meant to attract younger generations on Facebook. Challenges arose when tasked with coming up with engaging content while still remaining cautious of making any questionable statements and keeping all content formal.

On one particular post on Facebook, I covered the CBS Channel 8 interview with Public Watchdogs attorney, Chuck La Bella. I boosted the post, meaning I was able to gain more viewers by using Facebook segmentation algorithms. It was very successful in terms of engagement, but many commenters on Facebook did not click on the attached video and believed Public Watchdogs is a sort of anti-nuclear group. We received a lot of negative comments from people who are pro-nuclear. From then on, I made sure to be particularly cautious on social media to make it clear that Public Watchdogs is advocating against the unsafe storage practices of nuclear waste at SONGS, and not against nuclear waste in general. With Charles Langley's instruction, I learned how to effectively manage the negative comments on Facebook. Inspired by Eli Saslow's article on the spread of misinformation online, I recognized the need to create a post to counter some of the misinformation that was spread involving Public Watchdogs by creating an FAQ for Public Watchdogs dispelling the false accusations made on Facebook (Saslow, 2018). The FAQ has yet to be approved by the legal team, but will be posted on the Public Watchdogs website, and I will make a social media post linking to the site.

I spent a lot of time during my internship researching the issue of nuclear waste on government organization websites, such as the Nuclear Regulatory Commission (NRC.) Because of the nature of government and legal documents, it was time consuming for me to research issues and find information within the many pages and the technical jargon frequently used. It was incredibly valuable for me to take this dense material and break it down into information that the public could easily and quickly understand on social media and my other outputs posted on our website. It was a great challenge to explain events involving government organizations and corporations with long names and corresponding acronyms, and terms such as Independent Spent Fuel Storage Installation (ISFSI).

It was also a bit of a challenge for me to create content that appeals to a 60 year and older crowd on social media and other mediums. I do not have a lot of experience writing for, let alone reading, newspapers despite my extensive background in communications given my Advertising Management major and Environmental Communications Master's program. Creating content for the newspaper and media buying was an entirely new skill that I acquired while working for Public Watchdogs. It was also interesting to learn how to engage an age group with whom I do not have a lot of experience.

The understanding of Public Watchdogs' "social media network" was attempted in this internship in order to create different frames, and reach a wider range of people in the Southern California community (Fine and Kanter, 2010). During the process of understanding Public Watchdogs' complex social media network, I found certain "hubs" that helped us connect to "nodes" that existed more on the "edge of periphery" (Fine and Kanter, 2010). For example, I discovered that Adelia Sandoval, a spiritual spokesperson for the Acjachemen Nation, is a hub with multiple connections to other nearby indigenous communities. Working with her, and helping her to communicate the nuclear waste issue from an Acjachemen member's perspective strengthened Public Watchdogs connection with this hub and could later encourage involvement from nearby indigenous communities once the Acjachemen story angle is posted.

4. Acknowledgements

I would like to thank Charles Langley and Nina Babiarz for the opportunity to work at Public Watchdogs and for all of the dedication and time they each spent with me through the course of my internship. I am grateful to have learned from these two and to be a part of their team. I consider myself lucky to have had wise, considerate, approachable, and patient mentors advising me through this entire project.

I would like to thank former TV news anchor, Lynn Stewart, for working with me on social media and investing so much time and energy to help improve my skills.

I would like to thank Jennifer Moores, generous donor of Public Watchdogs, for providing the funds for the creation of my content and for believing in my work.

I would like to thank Dr. Meryl Shriver Rice, my advisor, for guiding me through this internship and being supportive through the process. The completion of this degree would not have been possible without her guidance.

I would like to thank my committee members Charles Langley, Dr. Meryl Shriver-Rice, Shara Pavlow and Dr. Michelle Seelig for investing the time in serving as committee members on my defense.

I would like to thank my parents, Miguel Alvarez and Lori Love, for supporting me throughout my graduate school program. I would also like to thank them for the countless sacrifices they have made to ensure that I had all the resources I needed to succeed.

I would like to thank my grandmother, Sharon Love, for being a constant source of support.

Lastly, I would like to thank my peers, Talia Horvath, Dana Biddle, Mollie Beek, Adam Roberty, and Sophie Cayuso for all of the encouragement and endless support. Getting the opportunity to know my peers and form these friendships was a valuable benefit of the Master's of Professional Science program at the University of Miami.

5.0 References Cited

Hansen, Anders, and J. Robert. Cox. Routledge Handbook of Environment and Communication. Routledge, 2015.

Pearson, Adam R., Matthew T. Ballew, Sarah Naiman, and Jonathon P. Schuldt. "Race, Class, Gender and Climate Change Communication." Oxford Research Encyclopedia of Climate Science, 2017. doi:10.1093/acrefore/9780190228620.013.412.

Saslow, Eli. "'Nothing on This Page Is Real': How Lies Become Truth in Online America." The

Washington Post. November 17, 2018. Accessed April 06, 2019 https://www.washingtonpost.com/national/nothing-on-this-page-is-real-how-lies-become-truthin-online-america/2018/11/17/edd44cc8-e85a-11e8-bbdb-72fdbf9d4fed_story.html.

Dunaway, Finis. Seeing Green: The Use and Abuse of American Environmental Images. Chicago: University of Chicago Press, 2015.

Kanter, Beth, and Allison H. Fine. The Networked Nonprofit: Connecting with Social Media to Drive Change. San Francisco: Jossey-Bass, 2010.

Shome, Debika, Sabine Marx, Kirstin Appelt, and Ian Webster. The Psychology of Climate Change Communication: A Guide for Scientists, Journalists, Educators, Political Aides, and the Interested Public. New York: Center for Research on Environmental Decisions, 2009.

Pezullo, P. C., & Cox, R. (n.d.). *Environmental Communication and the Public Sphere.*
"Public Watchdogs: Because the Public Has a Right to Know." Public Watchdogs: Because the Public Has a Right to Know. Accessed April 06, 2019. https://publicwatchdogs.org/.

Nuclear Power in the USA - World Nuclear Association, www.world-nuclear.org/information-library/country-profiles/countries-t-z/usa-nuclear-power.aspx.

https://publicwatchdogs.org/wp-content/uploads/2019/08/1-Complaint_Upload-09-04-2019-930AM.pdf

"San Onofre Safety." *San Onofre Safety*, sanonofresafety.org/.

http://marinemitigation.msi.ucsb.edu/documents/artificial_reef/annual_monitoring_reports/2017
_annualreport-SONGS_kelp_reef_mitigation.pdf

Stern. (n.d.). A value-belief-norm theory of support for social movements: The case of environmentalism. .

YOUR KNOWLEDGE HAS VALUE

- We will publish your bachelor's and
  master's thesis, essays and papers

- Your own eBook and book -
  sold worldwide in all relevant shops

- Earn money with each sale

Upload your text at www.GRIN.com
and publish for free